TULSA CITY-COUNTY LIBRARY

D0933173

Reading for TODAY

Workbook Two

PROGRAM AUTHORS

Linda Ward Beech • **Tara McCarthy**

PROGRAM CONSULTANTS

Myra K. Baum
Office of Adult and
    Continuing Education
Brooklyn, New York

Julie Jacobs
Inmate Literacy Project
Santa Clara County Library
Milpitas, California

Francis J. Feltman, Jr.
Racine Youth Offender
    Correctional Facility
Racine, Wisconsin

Maxine L. McCormick
Workforce Education
Orange County Public Schools
Orlando, Florida

Mary Ann Guilliams
Gary Job Corps
San Marcos, Texas

Sandra S. Owens
Laurens County Literacy Council
Laurens, South Carolina

STECK-VAUGHN
ELEMENTARY · SECONDARY · ADULT · LIBRARY

A Harcourt Company

www.steck-vaughn.com

Acknowledgments

STAFF CREDITS

Executive Editor: Ellen Northcutt

Senior Editor: Donna Townsend

Supervising Designer: Pamela Heaney

Designer: Jessica Bristow

ILLUSTRATION CREDITS: Scott Bieser, Holly Cooper, Joan Pilch

ISBN 0-7398-2954-8

Copyright © 2001 Steck-Vaughn Company

All rights reserved. No part of the material protected by this copyright may be reproduced or utilized in any form or by any means, electronic or mechanical, including photocopying, recording, or by any information storage and retrieval system, without permission in writing from the copyright owner. Requests for permission to make copies of any part of the work should be mailed to: Copyright Permissions, Steck-Vaughn Company, P.O. Box 26015, Austin, Texas 78755.

Printed in the United States of America

2 3 4 5 6 7 8 9 10 RP 04 03 02

Contents

To the Instructor

The *Reading for Today* Workbooks are designed to accompany the new structure of the *Reading for Today* Student Books. Books 1–6 have corresponding workbooks that follow the same format in:

- controlled vocabulary
- reading level
- phonics and word-building skills
- sight vocabulary
- writing and comprehension skills

Student Book ➡	Workbook
UNIT CONTENTS	**UNIT CONTENTS**
• Discussion	• Discussion
• Sight words	• Reading practice
• Phonics skills	• Phonics generalizations
• Writing skills	• Writing applications
• Reading selection	• Extended reading selection
• Comprehension questions	• Comprehension questions
• Life-coping Skills	• Writing practice

The chart shows how a typical unit in a *Reading for Today* workbook serves as a follow-up for its corresponding unit in a *Reading for Today* student book.

Students who use the *Reading for Today* Workbooks, however, do not simply review, practice, and reinforce sight words, phonics, and writing skills. Students also extend their learning. They read additional adult-related stories that are written with the controlled vocabulary that puts the reading within their grasp. Students discuss what they bring of their own experience to the reading selections by responding to purpose-setting questions, thus sharpening their thinking and discussion skills. And students write, both to demonstrate comprehension and to respond in their own way to the reading selections.

Teaching Suggestions

Each unit in the *Reading for Today* Workbooks follows the pattern outlined below.

Reading and Discussing Page 3

Objectives: To help the student see the connection between reading and speaking. To improve comprehension through discussion.

Teaching Steps:
A. Read the question or questions. Encourage the learner to talk about the question. Discussing the question will help the student get ready to read the story that follows.
B. Help the student read the story. Remember to praise the learner's efforts.
C. Talk about the story. Help the student answer the discussion question that follows the story. Reread the story if necessary.

Review Words · Page 4

Objective: To review the sight words introduced in previous units.

Teaching Steps: Be sure the student understands the directions for each exercise. Have students check their answers by referring to the Answer Key at the back of the book.

Sight Words · Page 5

Objectives: To review the sight words learned in the corresponding student book unit. To practice reading word groups or phrases rather than individual words.

Teaching Steps:
A. Help the student read and reread each phrase until each one is smooth and natural. Move your hand or a pencil in an arc under each phrase as the learner reads, to help "push" the reader toward fluency. Praise the learner's success.
B. Help the student fill in the blanks correctly.
C. Practice reading the entire story for fluency. Rereading the story after practicing the phrasing will give the learner a sense of success.

Phonics Practice · Pages 6 and 7

Objective: To review and reinforce the phonics skills taught in the student book.

Teaching Steps: Be sure the learner understands the directions for each exercise. Have students check their answers by referring to the Answer Key at the back of the book.

Writing Skills · Page 8

Objective: To review and reinforce the writing skills taught in the student book.

Teaching Steps: Help the learner understand the directions for each exercise. Have students check their answers by referring to the Answer Key at the back of the book.

Comprehension · Page 9

Objectives: To read the conclusion of the story and answer comprehension questions in writing.

Teaching Steps:
A. Have the student read the story.
B. Have the student write the answers to the questions. The following hints will help the learner succeed.
   1. The answer to the question may often be found stated directly in the story.
   2. Rereading the story after reading a question may make it easier to answer the question.
   3. Some questions can be answered by turning the question into a statement and completing the statement with the answer from the story.

From Reading to Writing · Page 10

Objectives: To give students an opportunity to write about their own lives or life experiences. To reinforce reading by writing something for someone else to read.

Teaching Steps:
A. Encourage the learner to get as many ideas or thoughts on paper as possible. Praise any legitimate attempts to write. Try for more clarity only as your student gains confidence in writing.
B. When your student finishes writing, you may wish to go back over the writing and follow the suggestions in Part B of each writing page.

Unit One

Managing Money

READING AND DISCUSSING

A. Talk about it.

Can you plan the use of money?
How well can you save money?

B. Read the story.

A Plan for Jan

Jan does well at work. She is lucky to have a fine boss. He tells Jan to plan some time with her family. This is her chance to go to her brother. He is in the country. She can go by bus.

Can Jan buy a bus ticket? She looks in her wallet. It looks like NO! Where does the money go? Jan does not have to ask. When she is in a store, she does not plan well. She buys and buys!

C. Think about it.

How can Jan save money?

A. Read the words. Write the first letter.

1. first fan ____f____

2. where _____

3. bills _____

4. have _____

5. does _____

6. sit _____

B. Read the words in the list. Write the words that fit in the sentences. Read the sentences.

brother
very
money
cannot
sits
bills

1. Jan _____ buy a bus ticket.

2. She has no _____ for it.

3. Her _____ are big.

4. Her _____ cannot help her.

5. Matt has not been _____ well.

6. He _____ and looks for Jan.

C. Write the word <u>bill</u> for each picture. Use a capital letter for a name.

1. This is a
____bill____.

2. It has a
_____.

3. This is
_____.

A. Read the phrases in the box aloud. Practice until you can read them smoothly.

1. has a lucky chance
2. sat and looked
3. money in her wallet
4. is upset
5. bus ticket
6. she plans
7. walk on by
8. cannot lose money

B. Write the phrases to complete the story.

Jan _____has a lucky chance_____ to go to the country.

1

She _____ at the

2

_____. She _____

3   4

that she cannot buy a _____. So,

5

_____ to save her money. She will

6

_____ the stores. She _____

7   8

_____ if she does not go in!

C. Read the story aloud. Practice until you can read it smoothly.

A. Read the words in the list. They all have the short a sound. Write other words with the short a sound. Read them.

an
ban
pan
man
plan
chance

1. r + an = _____ran_____

2. J + an = _____

3. f + an = _____

4. c + an = _____

5. v + an = _____

B. Read the word pairs aloud. Circle the words with the short a sound. Write them.

1. (tan)   ten   _____tan_____

2. can   cane   _____

3. bed   ban   _____

4. me   man   _____

5. on   an   _____

C. Read the sentences. Circle the words with the short a sound. Write them.

1. (Jan) works in a food store. _____Jan_____

2. Can she get to the country? _____

3. She has a plan to go by bus. _____ _____

4. This is a chance to see her brother. _____

5. He is a fine man. _____

Short a

pat
sat
rat
and
has
have

A. **Read the words in the list. They all have the short a sound. Write other words with the short a sound. Read them.**

1. h + at = _____

2. b + at = _____

3. th + at = _____

4. c + at = _____

5. m + at = _____

6. t + an = _____

B. **Read the word pairs aloud. Circle the words with the short a sound. Write them.**

1. have   home   _____

2. she   stand   _____

3. ran   run   _____

4. Jan   not   _____

5. sit   sat   _____

6. at   it   _____

C. **Read the sentences. Circle the words with the short a sound. Write them.**

1. Matt looks for his sister. _____

2. What can she save? _____

3. She makes a plan. _____

4. This is her chance for the bus ticket. _____

5. That is what she is working to buy. _____

Recognizing Sentences

A. Write the sentences to make them correct.

1. can Jan buy a ticket?

_____

2. she has a fine plan.

_____

3. save your money!

_____

B. Write each sentence. End it with the correct mark.

1. Look at that

_____

2. The wallet is fat

_____

3. Will she go to the store

_____

C. Write the sentences to make them correct.

1. the boss likes her work

_____

2. is the ticket in the wallet

_____

3. stop going to the store

_____

Comprehension

A. Read the rest of the story.

A Plan for Jan

Matt: I am lucky that you are with me, Jan. You plan your time well.

Jan: And today I plan my money well, Matt! The boss gave me this chance to be with you. But I had no money for a bus ticket. It was like my wallet had a hole in it. I was buying and buying!

Matt: But you got the bus ticket, Jan.

Jan: Yes, my plan to save money for tickets works fine. The plan is to walk on by the stores!

Matt: That plan is helping us both. You save money, and I get time with you!

B. Write the answers to the questions. Use complete sentences.

1. Why does Jan want to buy a bus ticket?

   _____

   _____

2. What plan does she make to save money?

   _____

   _____

3. How does her plan help Matt?

   _____

   _____

From Reading to Writing

A. Write your own story. You can use your own subject or find one in the box. You may want to use the phrases below in your story.

Subjects

Work	Plans	Bills
go to work	make a plan	paying bills
in a food store	go by bus	save money
have money	use money well	at the store
a fine boss	have a chance	in a wallet
get two jobs	buy a ticket	lose money

_____

_____

_____

_____

_____

_____

_____

_____

_____

_____

B. Read your story. Did you write in sentences? Did you begin and end each sentence correctly? Check to make sure.

READING AND DISCUSSING

A. Talk about it.

Are you working? Do you have a job in the city?

B. Read the story.

City Jobs

The people in this family are lucky. We got jobs in the city. Dan works with cars. He can get a car to go! Dot helps in a store. People buy lights and tables from her to use at home. Bill has a job at a food stand. I work at Radio KOY. I am on from seven to eight.

C. Think about it.

Is this family lucky to have city jobs?
Can you do a job like one of them has?

A. Read the words in the first list. Then write the words under the correct letter.

big
sister
city
she
brother
chance
home
her

b

big

_____

_____

c

_____

_____

s

_____

_____

h

_____

_____

B. Look down and across in the box. Find the words from the second list of words and circle them. Write them.

key
go
pays
desk
look
family

d	b	g	w	f	g
e	l	o	o	k	p
s	t	p	a	y	s
k	p	t	k	e	y
f	a	m	i	l	y

1. _key_ _____

2. _____

3. _____

4. _____

5. _____

6. _____

C. Write the word <u>work</u> for each picture.

1. They _____ well.

2. She is at _____.

3. This is her _____.

Sight Words

A. Read the phrases in the box aloud. Practice until you can read them smoothly.

1. My mother went
2. She got a job
3. She will have a chance
4. She loves
5. sends hats to people
6. for children
7. are bigger

B. Write the phrases to complete the story.

_____ to a hat store.

1

_____ at the store. _____

2   3

_____ to make hats for

money. _____ this work. This store

4

_____. The hats are

5

_____. Mother can make hats that

6

_____. She likes to make cute ones

7

for children.

C. Read the story aloud. Practice until you can read it smoothly.

13

A. Read the words in the list. They all have the short e sound. Write other words with the short e sound. Read them.

end
bed
ten
help
them
seven

1. s + end = _____

2. b + end = _____

3. y + ell = _____

4. l + end = _____

5. m + end = _____

B. Read the word pairs aloud. Circle the words with the short e sound. Write them.

1. yell   you   _____

2. he   help   _____

3. ten   tan   _____

4. well   we   _____

5. stand   seven   _____

6. desk   dad   _____

C. Read the sentences. Circle the words with the short e sound. Write them.

1. Mother can mend hats. _____

2. Her job ends at 6 P.M. _____

3. Dot helps in a store. _____

4. My mother makes hats to send to children. _____

5. I am on the radio from seven to eight. _____

A. **Read the words in the list. They all have the short e sound. Write other words with the short e sound. Read them.**

get
them
yell
bent
dent
sent

1. t + ent = _____

2. r + ent = _____

3. w + ell = _____

4. w + ent = _____

5. l + ent = _____

B. **Read the word pairs aloud. Circle the words with the short e sound. Write them.**

1. bill   bent   _____

2. end   eight   _____

3. ran   rent   _____

4. got   get   _____

5. they   ten   _____

6. work   went   _____

C. **Read the sentences. Circle the words with the short e sound. Write them.**

1. A woman got a dent in the car. _____

2. She sent the car to Dan. _____

3. People buy beds from Dot. _____

4. She works well with people. _____

5. People like Dot, and she likes to work with them.

_____

Adding –s, –ed, and -ing to Verbs

A. Add the ending. Write each new word. Read each new word.

	-s	**-ed**	**-ing**
1. yell	yells	yelled	yelling
2. rent	_____	_____	_____
3. help	_____	_____	_____
4. work	_____	_____	_____
5. end	_____	_____	_____

B. Read the sentences. Write the correct word in the blank.

Bill: Is Dot _____ to work?

                  go   going

Dan: She went. She _____ to work at eight.

                        walked   walking

She _____ to get to the store by nine.

          likes   liking

C. Read the paragraph. Circle the words that end in -s, -ed, or -ing.

My brother works at a food stand in the city. He is looking for a job in a store. A store job pays well. Dot is helping my brother look. She worked in a food store. The boss likes her. Dot sent my brother to this boss. It looks like he will have a chance to get a job at the bigger food store.

D. Write sentences using words ending in -s, -ed, or -ing.

1. _____

2. _____

3. _____

Comprehension

A. Read the rest of the story.

City Jobs

I have a job on the radio. I love this job! I am lucky to have it. My job pays well. The people at work have helped me, and the job is going well for me.

My family likes Radio KOY. They get home from work and sit by the radio. Dan yells to my mother and brother to stop working and sit with him. His sister is on the radio!

From seven to eight they have the radio on. They are my fans, and they love my work on the radio. We are a lucky family. We are going to make it in the city.

B. Write the answers to the questions. Use complete sentences.

1. Where is Jan working?

_____

_____

2. Can Jan make good money at her job?

_____

_____

3. Who are the fans Jan has?

_____

_____

4. Why is her family lucky?

_____

_____

A. Write your own story. You can use your own idea or find one in the box. You may want to use the phrases below in your story.

Subjects

Jobs	The City	The Radio
in the city	renting homes	for the family
money for us	cars, cars, cars	for children
going by bus	people and stores	fans like it
working on cars	not the country	by my bed
helping people	make it big	gets me going

_____

_____

_____

_____

_____

_____

_____

_____

_____

_____

B. Read your story. Did you tell all that you wanted to tell? Did you add the right endings? Go back and check all the action words.

READING AND DISCUSSING

A. Talk about it.

Do you smoke? Can you stop?

B. Read the story.

Walk On By

Kent: Stop that! You will get sick.

Luke: I will light one and stop.

Kent: From one you will go to two. From two you will go to three. It works like that.

Luke: No! I can stop at one.

Kent: Luke, my mother cannot stop. My sister cannot stop. You have a chance to stop. Walk on by!

C. Think about it.

Are you sick of smoking? Can you help people stop?

A. Look down and across in the box. Find the words from the first list of words and circle them. Write them.

like
of
chance
help
people
pay

p	c	h	a	n	c	e
r	p	e	o	p	l	e
g	y	l	i	k	e	o
h	v	p	a	y	z	f
b	d	j	k	m	q	x

1. _____
2. _____
3. _____
4. _____
5. _____
6. _____

B. Read the second list of words. Write the words that fit in the sentences. Read the sentences.

sick
plan
stop
me
lucky

1. I am _____ of smoking.

2. Can I _____ smoking?

3. I have to have a _____ to stop.

4. Kent will help _____.

5. I am _____ to have Kent to help me.

C. Write the word <u>have</u> for each picture.

1. We _____ a cat.

2. I _____ run.

3. I _____ to run.

Sight Words

A. Read the phrases in the box aloud. Practice until you can read them smoothly.

> 1. by a group
> 2. bets they are smoking
> 3. feels that
> 4. get bad health from doing this
> 5. at an ad
> 6. out to make people smoke
> 7. do what he can

B. Write the phrases to complete the story.

Kent and Luke walk _____. Kent

looks at them. He _____.

Kent _____ Luke will _____
3   4

_____.

Kent and Luke look _____. Is it
5

_____? No, this ad is out to
6

make people stop smoking. Luke will _____
7

_____ to stop smoking.

C. Read the story aloud. Practice until you can read it smoothly.

A. Read the words in the list. They all have the short <u>a</u> sound. Write other words with the short <u>a</u> sound. Read them.

ad

bad

van

hat

family

chance

1. d + ad = _____

2. c + an = _____

3. h + ad = _____

4. s + ad = _____

5. p + ad = _____

6. f + at = _____

B. Read the word pairs aloud. Circle the words with the short <u>a</u> sound. Write them.

1. mad   make   _____

2. run   ran   _____

3. it   at   _____

4. that   this   _____

5. help   have   _____

6. hat   hate   _____

C. Read the sentences. Circle the words with the short <u>a</u> sound. Write them.

1. Smoking makes Luke feel like a man. _____

2. He smokes and he feels big. _____

3. Will Luke get a chance to stop? _____

4. Kent feels bad for Luke. _____

5. This is a chance for Luke to stop. _____

Phonics   Short e

A. Read the words in the list. They all have the short e sound. Write other words with the short e sound. Read them.

jet
pet
well
them
send
seven

1. s + et   = _____

2. g + et   = _____

3. b + ent = _____

4. l + et   = _____

5. b + ed   = _____

B. Read the word pairs aloud. Circle the words with the short e sound. Write them.

1. bad   bed   _____

2. met   mat   _____

3. was   wet   _____

4. table   tent   _____

5. mend   money   _____

6. land   lend   _____

C. Read the sentences. Circle the words with the short e sound. Write them.

1. Kent has a big radio. _____

2. Can an ad on the radio help people stop smoking?

_____

3. Will the ad get Luke to stop? _____

4. Luke bets he will stop. _____

5. Yet, Luke likes to smoke with the group. _____

Using Contractions

A. Read the contractions and write them.

1. I am = I'm

_____

2. they will = they'll

_____

3. I will = I'll

_____

4. cannot = can't

_____

5. she is = she's

_____

6. it is = it's

_____

B. Rewrite each sentence to make the underlined words a contraction.

1. <u>I will</u> stop smoking.

I'll stop smoking. _____

2. <u>I am</u> lucky to have Kent.

_____

3. <u>It is</u> big of him to help me.

_____

4. <u>He is</u> helping me with my health.

_____

C. Read the paragraph. Circle the contractions.

Smoking can't make me a big man. It's a ticket to bad health for me. I'll get out. I'll stop. I'm not going to get sick from smoking. The group will not stop. They'll be no help to me. Kent will help me. He's on my side. I'm going to get out of the group.

Comprehension

A. Read the rest of the story.

Walk On By

Rob: Luke, I have a light for you.

Luke: No, Rob. I'm not smoking.

Rob: You can't do that, man! This group smokes.
       I smoke, Van smokes, Pat smokes.

Kent: Well, Luke is going to stop.

Rob: You are like my mother, Kent. Smoking is not
       bad. We like it in this group.

Kent: Smoking is for zeros, Rob. Luke is not one
       of them.

Rob: Go for a walk, Kent. You make me sick.

Luke: I'll go with him.

Rob: Luke, stop! Look! This one is for you.

Luke: No, I can't go on smoking. I'll see you, Rob.

B. Write the answers to the questions. Use complete sentences.

1. Is Rob helping Luke?

_____

_____

2. Why was Rob mad at Kent?

_____

_____

3. Who helps Luke in the end? Why?

_____

_____

From Reading to Writing

A. Write your own story. You can use your own idea or find one in the box. You may want to use the phrases below in your story.

Subjects

Smoking	Health	Bad Groups
can you stop	ads can help	bad for you
get out	sick in bed	run out on you
feeling bad	food and water	stop going with
can't stand it	jobs for nurses	look out for them
uses money	get well	do not get in one

_____

_____

_____

_____

_____

_____

_____

_____

_____

_____

_____

B. Read your story. Take out words you don't like. Add words you do like. Did you write your contractions correctly? Go back and check.

Unit Four

Using Leisure Time

READING AND DISCUSSING

A. Talk about it.

Do you have chances to go out with the family?

B. Read the story.

Out with the Family

Bill and I work from nine to five, yet we have chances to go out with the children. We feel lucky. The children love to go out with us.

The six of us get on a bus. We set out to look at the city. We get out and walk. We feel that it helps the children to look at people, homes, and big stores. Bill and I talk with the children, and they talk with us. Our family is a group that gets on well.

C. Think about it.

Is a family like this a good group to be with?

A. Read the words in the list. Read the phrases. Write the word that tells about it.

us
two
food
table
sister
brother
mother
family
bigger
children

1. buy it at a store _____food_____

2. a woman with children _____

3. one and one _____

4. you and me _____

5. a group of people at home _____

6. A van is a _____ car.

7. We set food on the _____.

8. A mother loves her _____.

9. two people in a family _____

_____

B. Write <u>was</u> or <u>with</u> on each line. Read the sentences.

1. I am _____ my family.

2. My brother is _____ my mother.

3. _____ my mother in the car with him?

4. She _____ _____ him.

5. Where _____ my sister?

C. Write sentences using the review words.

1. _____

2. _____

3. _____

Sight Words

A. Read the phrases in the box aloud. Practice until you can read them smoothly.

> 1. to go out with our children
> 2. On one holiday
> 3. to eat
> 4. fed us some good food
> 5. that my mother is tops
> 6. to talk and be with her
> 7. talks to Mother
> 8. for a holiday

B. Write the phrases to complete the story.

We love _____.
                        1

_____, Bill and the children and
          2

I went _____ with my mother. She
               3

_____. My children
                    4

feel _____. They love
                        5

_____. My brother
                    6

_____ when he can.
                7

Mother loves to have both her children at home

_____.
        8

C. Read the story aloud. Practice until you can read it smoothly.

A. **Read the words in the list. They all have the short o sound. Write other words with the short o sound. Read them.**

mop
cop
holiday
job
stop
not

1. t + op = _____

2. p + op = _____

3. g + ot = _____

4. h + op = _____

5. l + ot = _____

6. r + ob = _____

B. **Read the word pairs aloud. Circle the words with the short o sound. Write them.**

1. Jan   job   _____

2. home   hop   _____

3. smoke   stop   _____

4. not   no   _____

5. top   to   _____

6. get   got   _____

C. **Read the sentences. Circle the words with the short o sound. Write them.**

1. Pop is in a home. _____

2. He is not well. _____

3. We hope this holiday feels good to him. _____

4. We stop in to be with him. _____

5. We like to be with my dad a lot. _____

A. **Read the words in the list. They all have the short e sound. Write other words with the short e sound. Read them.**

fed
Ted
get
help
ten
well

1. b + ed = _____

2. r + ent = _____

3. r + ed = _____

4. l + et = _____

5. m + end = _____

6. w + ed = _____

B. **Read the word pairs aloud. Circle the words with the short e sound. Write them.**

1. led   love   _____

2. eight   Jed   _____

3. feel   fed   _____

4. went   we   _____

5. be   bend   _____

6. she   send   _____

C. **Read the sentences. Circle the words with the short e sound. Write them.**

1. Ned is my brother. _____

2. He helps us on holidays. _____

3. My brother gets the food. _____

4. Ned let us have the holiday at his home.

_____   _____

5. I bet no one has a brother like him! _____

Using Contractions

A. Draw lines to match the words with the contractions. Then read the contractions.

1. was not   **a.** I've

2. is not   **b.** wasn't

3. we are   **c.** we'll

4. we will   **d.** isn't

5. I have   **e.** don't

6. do not   **f.** we're

B. The contraction for <u>will</u> <u>not</u> is <u>won't</u>. Write <u>won't</u> to complete the sentences. Read the sentences.

1. I _____ be home for the holiday.

2. I _____ be with my family.

3. It _____ be a good holiday for me.

C. Write the contractions. Then read the story.

My brother Ned _____ be with us for the
                        cannot

holiday. This holiday _____ a good one for him.
                        is not

_____ talk with him from home. _____
  We will   **I have**

got lots of love to send him. We _____ get to see
                                do not

him a lot. _____ lucky we can talk with him
            We are

from time to time.

Comprehension

A. Read the rest of the story.

Out with the Family

Nan: We love this chance to talk with you, Ned! Is the holiday OK for you?

Ned: It isn't that good, Nan. I'm out on this job in the country, and I can't get home to you and Bill and the children and Mother.

Nan: It isn't good for us with you not at home.

Ned: Is Pop OK? Have you looked in on him?

Nan: Bill and the children and I went to talk to him. He sends you his love.

Bill: That job you have isn't the one for me, Ned. On a holiday, it feels good to be with the family.

Ned: The group I work with is like a family, Bill. We can't be in our homes for the holiday, yet we'll eat and talk and do OK. You can make a family out of the people you are with.

Nan: The children and Mother send love to you.

Bill: Go on with the good work, Ned.

Ned: OK, brother. Have a good holiday!

B. Write the answers to the questions. Use complete sentences.

1. Why isn't Ned with his family on the holiday?

_____

_____

2. What is Ned doing on this holiday?

_____

_____

A. Write your own story. You can use your own idea or find one in the box. You may want to use the phrases below in your story.

Subjects

Holidays	Food	Children
to go out	good for you	a big family
my group	for my health	a lot of love
talk a lot	on the table	help with the food
feel good	help out	brothers and sisters
on the job	eat a lot	a good mother and dad

_____

_____

_____

_____

_____

_____

_____

_____

_____

_____

B. Read your story. You may want to add words or take some words out. Did you use contractions in your story? Make sure you spelled them correctly.

Job Safety

READING AND DISCUSSING

A. Talk about it.

What are some jobs people do at home for pay?

B. Read the story.

A Job at Home

Ken: I have the plans for fixing up our home for the children. Do you like the plans? Are they OK?

Olive: They look good, but let's talk about them. When I have a group of children in my home, they have to be safe. I can't make mistakes and get in trouble.

Ken: I have looked at the city health and safety rules for people like us who work at home.

Olive: Ken, I will run a good, safe home for the children. When can I get going?

C. Think about it.

What job is Olive going to do?
Why can't she take chances on safety?

A. Look down and across in the box. Find the words from the first list of words and circle them. Write them.

do
feel
plan
help
water
health

c	r	f	m	i	w	b
v	h	e	l	p	a	c
w	h	e	a	l	t	h
g	t	l	u	a	e	k
u	d	o	f	n	r	z

1. _____

2. _____

3. _____

4. _____

5. _____

6. _____

B. Read the words in the second list. Read the phrases. Write the word in or after the phrase that tells about it.

lucky
group
table
bills
nurse
can't

1. a man or woman who helps sick people _____

2. money you have to pay _____

3. You can sit at a _____.

4. You can have fun with people in a _____.

5. I like olives, but I _____ eat them.

6. I was _____ I wasn't hurt.

C. Write the word <u>help</u> for each picture.

1. I can get

_____.

2. Can I

_____ you?

3. We _____

fix the food.

Sight Words

A. Read the phrases in the box aloud. Practice until you can read them smoothly.

1. use the safety rules
2. children get hurt
3. but they
4. out of trouble
5. her eyes on them
6. her glasses
7. for mistakes
8. a hand
9. talked about

B. Write the phrases to complete the story.

Olive will ———————————— in her home.
                    1

She doesn't plan to have ————————————.
                            2

Children can have fun, ——————— have to be
                          3

safe. Olive will keep the children ———————
                                      4

——————— by keeping ————————————.
                        5

Olive got ———————————————. She
              6

looked at the plan ———————————. Ken had
                      7

——————— in helping her. They ———————
    8   9

——————— the plan.

C. Read the story aloud. Practice until you can read it smoothly.

up
us
run
but
cut
lucky

A. Read the words in the list. They all have the short <u>u</u> sound. Write other words with the short <u>u</u> sound. Read them.

1. g + ut = _____

2. b + us = _____

3. n + ut = _____

4. h + ut = _____

5. r + ut = _____

6. c + up = _____

B. Read the word pairs aloud. Circle the words with the short <u>u</u> sound. Write them.

1. use   us   _____

2. group   gut   _____

3. run   ran   _____

4. nut   no   _____

5. cat   cut   _____

6. but   bet   _____

C. Read the sentences. Circle the words with the short <u>u</u> sound. Write them.

1. Olive feels lucky to have Ken help her. _____

2. She will run a good home for children. _____

3. Olive has her work cut out for her. _____

4. Her home is not big, but it is safe. _____

5. The bus stop is by her home. _____

A. **Read the words in the list. They all have the short a sound. Write other words with the short a sound. Read them.**

an
sad
that
land
stand
family

1. s + and = _____

2. p + ad = _____

3. f + an = _____

4. b + at = _____

5. h + and = _____

B. **Read the word pairs aloud. Circle the words with the short a sound. Write them.**

1. stand   stop   _____

2. but   bat   _____

3. send   sand   _____

4. tan   time   _____

5. and   end   _____

6. safe   sat   _____

C. **Read the sentences. Circle the words with the short a sound. Write them.**

1. What is the plan Olive has for the children?

_____ _____

2. She has good food for the children to eat. _____

3. Olive got a box with sand for them to dig in. _____

4. The children can run. _____

5. They will have a lot of fun. _____

A. Write the words. Start the names with a capital letter.

1. Olive _____   2. Ken _____

3. our _____   4. Pat _____

B. Write the sentences. Start with a capital letter.

1. Olive was a nurse.

  _____

2. She loves children.

  _____

3. This will be a good job for her.

  _____

C. Circle the letters that should be capital letters. Write the sentences correctly.

1. olive can help working people.

  _____

2. she can do this job well.

  _____

3. people will pay olive.

  _____

4. kim webb and i will take our children to olive.

  _____

  _____

A. Read the rest of the story.

A Job at Home

Olive: It's 9 A.M.—time to talk to Miss Rand from the city.

Ken: Let her in.

Olive: Do we have mats for nap time?

Ken: They are in this bin.

Olive: Did you mend the top of the table? Is it safe?

Ken: It's OK. The children can eat at it and work at it. No one will get hurt.

Olive: Do the lights work? Is the safety glass in?

Ken: Olive, stop it. Are you going to let Miss Rand in or not? We have met the safety rules for the city.

• • •

Ken: Is it 10 A.M. yet? That went well. Miss Rand liked what we did. She gave us the OK.

Olive: Good. We are set to go. Let's talk to some mothers and dads and get some children in our group.

B. Write the answers to the questions. Use complete sentences.

1. How did Olive feel at 9 A.M.?

_____

2. What will Olive and Ken do next?

_____

From Reading to Writing

A. Write your own story. You can use your own idea or find one in the box. You may want to use the phrases below in your story.

Subjects

Health and Safety	Working at Home	Plans
good safety plan	for some people	talk about them
to help people	at a desk	group health
at home and work	help the children	get help to make them
eat well	no boss	not by chance
not being sick or hurt	run an ad	good for work

_____

_____

_____

_____

_____

_____

_____

_____

_____

_____

_____

B. Read your story. Check to see if the names and sentences start with capital letters.

READING AND DISCUSSING

A. Talk about it.

Who or what makes you feel good? Why?

B. Read the story.

Ask T. J.

It was six A.M. and T. J. was on his bus. T. J. had a lot of fun on his job. He helped people get where they wanted to go. And he made them feel good on his bus.

Bix got on at the first stop. He asked T. J. about their city team. Did it win? Yes! T. J. and Bix did a hands up. Some children got on the bus at the second stop. One kid, Fay, looked sad. T. J. asked what the trouble was. They talked. In no time, T. J. made Fay laugh.

C. Think about it.

What is T. J. like?

A. Read the words in the list. Then write the words under the correct letter.

talk
seven
bus
well
water
stand
for
walk
nurse
we're
help

S

_____   _____

W

_____   _____

_____   _____

B. Look at the words in the list. Write the words that fit in the sentences. Read the sentences.

1. He can h_____ people.

2. She can t_____ to him.

3. She looks f_____ him.

4. She gets on the b_____.

5. T. J. is in the bus at s_____.

C. Write the word <u>light</u> for each picture.

1. She is

_____.

2. It is

_____

out.

3. She will

_____

it.

Sight Words

A. **Read the phrases in the box aloud. Practice until you can read them smoothly.**

> 1. makes friends
> 2. of all ages
> 3. old people
> 4. laugh a lot
> 5. like kin
> 6. did not have his glasses
> 7. to read

B. **Write the phrases to complete the story.**

T. J. _____ with people
_____1_____

_____ on his bus. He can make both
_____2_____

_____ and children _____.
_____3_____   _____4_____

T. J. is _____ to people. One time, Bix
_____5_____

_____ and
_____6_____

asked T. J. _____ to him!
_____7_____

C. **Read the story aloud. Practice until you can read it smoothly.**

A. Read the words in the list. They all have the short i sound. Write other words with the short i sound. Read them.

in
sin
bin
kin
him
with

1. d + in = _____

2. w + in = _____

3. b + ig = _____

4. s + it = _____

5. w + ill = _____

6. s + ick = _____

B. Read the word pairs aloud. Circle the words with the short i sound. Write them.

1. six   like   _____

2. find   fit   _____

3. light   Lin   _____

4. pin   pan   _____

5. fifth   file   _____

6. tin   ten   _____

C. Read the sentences. Circle the words with the short i sound. Write them.

1. Nine people sit on the bus. _____

2. They got on it at seven. _____

3. What will T. J. tell them today? _____

4. T. J. works well with people. _____

5. He is very good at this job. _____ _____

A. Read the words in the list. They all have the short o sound.
Write other words with the short o sound. Read them.

lot

pot

not

jobs

stop

boss

1. h + ot = _____

2. d + ot = _____

3. c + op = _____

4. c + ot = _____

5. j + ot = _____

6. m + op = _____

B. Read the word pairs aloud. Circle the words with the short o
sound. Write them.

1. got   go   _____

2. cot   cone   _____

3. do   dot   _____

4. home   hot   _____

5. jot   jet   _____

6. rob   robe   _____

C. Read the sentences. Circle the words with the short o sound.
Write them.

1. The bus stops at a home for old people. _____

2. It is not hot in the bus. _____ _____

3. That man has a lot to tote. _____

4. He has a big box. _____

5. T. J. hops up to help him. _____

A. Read the phrases in the box. Then write each one on the line next to the phrase that is the same.

a friend's desk	a dog's bed
the man's bus	the woman's laugh

1. the bed of a dog _____

2. the desk of a friend _____

3. the laugh of the woman _____

4. the bus of the man _____

B. Add 's when you write the word. Read the phrase.

1. _____ boss
        Bud

2. the _____ home
          group

3. the _____ kin
          mother

4. the _____ job
          man

C. Read the sentences. Write the word and add 's.

T. J. finds _____ wallet on the bus. He finds
                Lin

_____ umbrella. He looks for a _____
     Jack   **nurse**

hat and a _____ bone. People lose a lot on
              dog

his bus!

Comprehension

A. Read the rest of the story.

Ask T. J.

Will the sun be out today? Is it the time to take an umbrella? Ask T. J. He gets up at five to find out so he can tell the people on his bus.

Did the home team win or lose? Was it by a lot? Ask T. J. He tunes in on the radio to find out. He likes to tell people how their team did.

Tip Hanes was out sick for six days. When he was well and got on the bus to go to work, T. J. gave him a big hug. That made Tip feel very good.

Jan Fox had a bad time at work one day. She was fed up and mad. T. J. made her laugh. Jan wasn't so upset when she got home.

Why is T. J. like this? He feels that it is all in the job. People all have troubles and make mistakes. But no one likes to be sad all the time. So T. J. helps them have fun when they are on his bus. And he has fun with them. For T. J., that makes work like a good holiday.

B. Write the answers to the questions. Use complete sentences.

1. How does T. J. help people?

_____

_____

_____

2. How does T. J. feel about his work?

_____

_____

From Reading to Writing

A. Write your own story. You can use your own idea or find one in the box. You may want to use the phrases below in your story.

Subjects

Work	Friends	On a Bus
do it well	to help out	stand or sit
make money	feel good	at a bus stop
a good job	out in a car	read the ads
have fun at it	laugh a lot	look at people
help people	an old friend	when it's hot

_____

_____

_____

_____

_____

_____

_____

_____

_____

_____

_____

B. Read your story. You may want to make some of the sentences longer. Are there words in your story that should have 's added to them? Check your spelling.

READING AND DISCUSSING

A. Talk about it.

Do all people have jobs they like?

B. Read the story.

My Sister and Work

My sister has a job in a store, but it's not a job she likes. By the time she gets home she feels mad. She sits by the TV. She talks about the bad time she has with her boss and with the people she works with. Her job is a big zero to her.

Fay can't stop working. She gets good pay, and the money helps at home. Can't she get a job she likes? She looks for a job like that, but has no luck. It's not good for her to feel like this.

C. Think about it.

You are Fay's friend. Can you help her with her troubles at work?

Review Words

A. Read the words in the first list. Then write each one next to the words that begin with the same sound.

read
good
band
mother
lose
home
plan
this

1. bend   bin   ___band___

2. get   gut   _____

3. mop   met   _____

4. play   plane   _____

5. rut   rent   _____

6. hands   hot   _____

7. led   light   _____

8. that   the   _____

B. Read the words in the second list. Write the words that fit in the sentences. Read the sentences.

good
chance
group
trouble
mistakes
plans

1. Fay works with a big _____ of people.

2. She has _____ with them.

3. She makes a lot of _____ on the job.

4. Her boss feels that she has a _____ to do well.

5. He _____ to talk to her.

6. Fay has a _____ boss.

C. Write sentences using the review words.

1. _____

2. _____

3. _____

Sight Words

A. Read the phrases in the box aloud. Practice until you can read them smoothly.

> 1. likes music
> 2. He and his son
> 3. can play the guitar
> 4. fits in with the band
> 5. has a lot of fun
> 6. is finding friends
> 7. boss and his son

B. Write the phrases to complete the story.

Fay's boss _____. _____
                    1   2

_____ have a band. Fay _____
                                          3

_____. She _____
                          4

_____ and she _____
                              5

_____. Fay _____
                          6

_____ and doing well at her job in the store.

The _____ like Fay's guitar playing.
         7

C. Read the story aloud. Practice until you can read it smoothly.

A. **Read the words in the list. They all have the short u̲ sound.**
Write other words with the short u̲ sound. Read them.

fun

nun

bun

nut

us

cut

1. r + un = _____

2. r + ut = _____

3. s + un = _____

4. g + ut = _____

5. p + un = _____

6. h + ut = _____

B. **Read the word pairs aloud. Circle the words with the short u̲**
sound. Write them.

1. fan   fun   _____

2. group   gun   _____

3. nun   nurse   _____

4. nut   no   _____

5. sand   sun   _____

6. bat   but   _____

C. **Read the sentences. Circle the words with the short u̲ sound.**
Write them.

1. Our band is a lot of fun. _____

2. We work a lot, but we like it. _____

3. We don't get in a rut. _____

4. Stan runs the band. _____

5. He helps us with our music. _____

A. **Read the words in the list. They all have the short i sound. Write other words with the short i sound. Read them.**

in
bit
kit
sit
him
quit

1. f + it = _____

2. l + it = _____

3. b + ig = _____

4. w + ill = _____

5. h + it = _____

6. p + in = _____

B. **Read the word pairs aloud. Circle the words with the short i sound. Write them.**

1. pit   pet   _____

2. it's   I'll   _____

3. dent   did   _____

4. light   lit   _____

5. fit   five   _____

6. bet   bit   _____

C. **Read the sentences. Circle the words with the short i sound. Write them.**

1. People like this band. _____

2. I play with them a lot. _____

3. We play old-time hits. _____

4. I'm in a good group. _____

5. The band is tops. _____

Doubling a Letter
To Add –ed and -ing

A. **To write the word, double the last letter and add the ending.**

–ed		-ing	
1. pop _____		**1.** let _____	
2. ban _____		**2.** fan _____	
3. jot _____		**3.** mop _____	
4. tan _____		**4.** pat _____	
5. stop _____		**5.** plan _____	

B. **Add -ing in the correct way to the words below in the sentences. Then read the sentences.**

> **let   fit   sit   get**

1. The band is l_____ me play with them.

2. I am f_____ in with the band.

3. I am s_____ in with them.

4. I am g_____ a lot of fun from this.

C. **Add –ed in the correct way to the words below in the sentences. Then read the sentences.**

> **hop   plan   stop   ban**

1. People h_____ to the music.

2. We p_____ our music for them.

3. The music st_____ from time to time.

4. Our music will not be b_____.

A. Read the rest of the story.

My Sister and Work

Fay is working out her troubles. She wasn't doing well on her job. She did not get on well with her boss. She talked about her troubles all the time. It was no fun to be with her.

Fay and her boss have a talk. The boss feels that Fay can do OK on the job, but she will have to work at it. In the talk, Fay and her boss find out they both love music. The boss and his son have a band, and Fay loves music.

Fay and her boss talked about his band. They laughed and had a good time. They didn't talk about Fay's work troubles at all.

This talk led to a chance for Fay to play in Mr. Lake's band. Playing with the group helped Fay feel that she fit in, both on the job and with the band. Fay stopped feeling bad about her job. She stopped a lot of her mistakes on the job. She got a chance and did not quit.

B. Write the answers to the questions. Use complete sentences.

1. What did Fay and her boss both like?

_____

_____

2. Why did Fay stop a lot of her mistakes on the job?

_____

_____

_____

From Reading to Writing

A. Write your own story. You can use your own idea or find one in the box. You may want to use the phrases below in your story.

Subjects

Music	Troubles	The Boss
feeling good	working at them	getting on
in the band	don't quit	doing well
playing for fun	get some help	being on time
letting go	talking about them	find out about the job
good times	we all make mistakes	works with people

_____

_____

_____

_____

_____

_____

_____

_____

_____

_____

_____

B. Read your story. Is it as good as you can make it? Did you add the correct endings to your verbs? Did you spell them correctly? Go back and check.

Answer Key

Unit One

Page 4 **A.** 1 .f 2. w 3. b 4. h 5. d 6. s
B. 1. cannot 2. money 3. bills 4. brother
5. very 6. sits **C.** 1. bill 2. bill 3. Bill

Page 5 **B.** 1. has a lucky chance 2. sat and
looked. 3. money in her wallet. 4. is upset
5. bus ticket 6. she plans 7. walk on by
8. cannot lose money

Page 6 **A.** 1. ran 2. Jan 3. fan 4. can
5. van **B.** 1. tan 2. can 3. ban 4. man 5. an
C. 1. Jan 2. Can 3. has, plan 4. chance 5. man

Page 7 **A.** 1. hat 2. bat 3. that 4. cat
5. mat 6. tan **B.** 1. have 2. stand 3. ran
4. Jan 5. sat 6. at **C.** 1. Matt 2. can 3. plan
4. chance 5. that

Page 8 **A.** 1. Can Jan buy a ticket? 2. She
has a fine plan. 3. Save your money!
B. 1. Look at that! 2. The wallet is fat. 3. Will
she go to the store? **C.** 1. The boss likes her
work. 2. Is the ticket in the wallet? 3. Stop
going to the store!

Page 9 **B.** 1. She wants to visit her brother
in the country. 2. She plans to stay out of
stores. 3. He gets to spend more time with her.

Unit Two

Page 12 **A.** big, brother; city, chance;
sister, she; home, her **B.** Order may vary.
1. key 2. go 3. pays 4. desk 5. look
6. family **C.** 1. work 2. work 3. work

Page 13 **B.** 1. My mother went 2. She got
a job 3. She will have a chance 4. She loves
5. sends hats to people 6. for children
7. are bigger

Page 14 **A.** 1. send 2. bend 3. yell 4. lend
5. mend **B.** 1. yell 2. help 3. ten 4. well
5. seven 6. desk **C.** 1. mend 2. ends 3. helps
4. send 5. seven

Page 15 **A.** 1. tent 2. rent 3. well 4. went
5. lent **B.** 1. bent 2. end 3. rent 4. get 5. ten
6. went **C.** 1. dent 2. sent 3. beds 4. well
5. them

Page 16 **A.** 1. yells, yelled, yelling 2. rents,
rented, renting 3. helps, helped, helping
4. works, worked, working 5. ends, ended,
ending **B.** going, walked, likes **C.** works,
looking, pays, helping, worked, likes, looks
D. Discuss your sentences with your instructor.

Page 17 **B.** 1. Jan is working at Radio
KOY. 2. Yes, Jan can make good money at
her job. **B.** 3. Her brothers and mother are
her fans. 4. Her family is lucky because they
all have jobs, and they are going to make it
in the city.

Unit Three

Page 20 **A.** Order may vary. 1. like 2. of
3. chance 4. help 5. people 6. pay **B.** 1. sick
2. stop 3. plan 4. me 5. lucky **C.** 1. have
2. have 3. have

Page 21 **B.** 1. by a group 2. bets they are
smoking 3. feels that 4. get bad health from
doing this 5. at an ad 6. out to make people
smoke 7. do what he can

Page 22 **A.** 1. dad 2. can 3. had 4. sad
5. pad 6. fat **B.** 1. mad 2. ran 3. at 4. that
5. have 6. hat **C.** 1. man 2. and 3. chance
4. bad 5. chance

Page 23 **A.** 1. set 2. get 3. bent 4. let
5. bed **B.** 1. bed 2. met 3. wet 4. tent
5. mend 6. lend **C.** 1. Kent 2. help 3. get
4. bets 5. Yet

Page 24 **A.** 1. I'm 2. they'll 3. I'll 4. can't
5. she's 6. it's **B.** 1. I'll stop smoking. 2. I'm
lucky to have Kent. 3. It's big of him to help
me. 4. He's helping me with my health.
C. can't, It's, I'll, I'll, I'm, They'll, He's, I'm

Page 25 **B.** 1. No, Rob had a light for Luke.
2. Rob is mad at Kent for helping Luke stop
smoking. 3. Kent helps Luke because
smoking is bad for Luke's health.

Unit Four

Page 28 **A.** 1. food 2. mother 3. two 4. us
5. family 6. bigger 7. table 8. children *or*
family 9. brother, sister, *or* mother **B.** 1. with
2. with 3. Was 4. was, with 5. was **C.** Discuss
your sentences with your instructor.

Page 29 **B.** 1. to go out with our children
2. On one holiday 3. to eat 4. fed us some
good food 5. that my mother is tops 6. to
talk and be with her 7. talks to Mother
8. for a holiday

Page 30 **A.** 1. top 2. pop 3. got 4. hop 5. lot 6. rob **B.** 1. job 2. hop 3. stop 4. not 5. top 6. got **C.** 1. Pop 2. not 3. holiday 4. stop 5. lot

Page 31 **A.** 1. bed 2. rent 3. red 4. let 5. mend 6. wed **B.** 1. led 2. Jed 3. fed 4. went 5. bend 6. send **C.** 1. Ned 2. helps 3. gets 4. Ned, let 5. bet

Page 32 **A.** 1. b 2. d 3. f 4. c 5. a 6. e **B.** 1. won't 2. won't 3. won't **C.** can't, isn't, We'll, I've, don't, We're

Page 33 **B.** 1. Ned isn't with his family because he is on a job in the country. 2. Ned is spending the holiday with the group that he works with.

Unit Five

Page 36 **A.** Order may vary. 1. do 2. feel 3. plan 4. help 5. water 6. health **B.** 1. nurse 2. bills 3. table 4. group 5. can't 6. lucky **C.** 1. help 2. help 3. help

Page 37 **B.** 1. use the safety rules 2. children get hurt 3. but they 4. out of trouble 5. her eyes on them 6. her glasses 7. for mistakes 8. a hand 9. talked about

Page 38 **A.** 1. gut 2. bus 3. nut 4. hut 5. rut 6. cup **B.** 1. us 2. gut 3. run 4. nut 5. cut 6. but **C.** 1. lucky 2. run 3. cut 4. but 5. bus

Page 39 **A.** 1. sand 2. pad 3. fan 4. bat 5. hand **B.** 1. stand 2. bat 3. sand 4. tan 5. and 6. sat **C.** 1. plan, has 2. has 3. sand 4. can 5. have

Page 40 **A.** 1. Olive 2. Ken 3. our 4. Pat **B.** 1. Olive was a nurse. 2. She loves children. 3. This will be a good job for her. **C.** 1. Olive can help working people. 2. She can do this job well. 3. People will pay Olive. 4. Kim Webb and I will take our children to Olive.

Page 41 **B.** 1. At 9 A.M. Olive was nervous. 2. They will talk to some mothers and dads and get some children in their group.

Unit Six

Page 44 **A.** seven, stand; well, water, walk, we're **B.** 1. help 2. talk 3. for 4. bus 5. seven **C.** 1. light 2. light 3. light

Page 45 **B.** 1. makes friends 2. of all ages 3. old people 4. laugh a lot 5. like kin 6. did not have his glasses 7. to read

Page 46 **A.** 1. din 2. win 3. big 4. sit 5. will 6. sick **B.** 1. six 2. fit 3. Lin 4. pin 5. fifth 6. tin **C.** 1. sit 2. it 3. will 4. with 5. is, this

Page 47 **A.** 1. hot 2. dot 3. cop 4. cot 5. jot 6. mop **B.** 1. got 2. cot 3. dot 4. hot 5. jot 6. rob **C.** 1. stops 2. not, hot 3. lot 4. box 5. hops

Page 48 **A.** 1. a dog's bed 2. a friend's desk 3. the woman's laugh 4. the man's bus **B.** 1. Bud's 2. group's 3. mother's 4. man's **C.** Lin's, Jack's, nurse's, dog's

Page 49 **B.** 1. He gives them the weather and sports report, greets them happily, and talks to them. 2. He enjoys it and has a sunny, positive attitude.

Unit Seven

Page 52 **A.** 1. band 2. good 3. mother 4. plan 5. read 6. home 7. lose 8. this **B.** 1. group 2. trouble 3. mistakes 4. chance 5. plans 6. good **C.** Discuss your sentences with your instructor.

Page 53 **B.** 1. likes music 2. He and his son 3. can play the guitar 4. fits in with the band 5. has a lot of fun 6. is finding friends 7. boss and his son

Page 54 **A.** 1. run 2. rut 3. sun 4. gut 5. pun 6. hut **B.** 1. fun 2. gun 3. nun 4. nut 5. sun 6. but **C.** 1. fun 2. but 3. rut 4. runs 5. us

Page 55 **A.** 1. fit 2. lit 3. big 4. will 5. hit 6. pin **B.** 1. pit 2. it's 3. did 4. lit 5. fit 6. bit **C.** 1. this 2. with 3. hits 4. in 5. is

Page 56 **A.** 1. popped 2. banned 3. jotted 4. tanned 5. stopped; 1. letting 2. fanning 3. mopping 4. patting 5. planning **B.** 1. letting 2. fitting 3. sitting 4. getting **C.** 1. hopped 2. planned 3. stopped 4. banned

Page 57 **B.** 1. Fay and her boss both liked music. 2. Fay stopped a lot of her mistakes on the job because she began to feel that she fit in.